HAL•LEONARD INSTRUMENTAL PLAY-ALONG

HORN

STEPHEN SONDHEIM BROADWAY SOLOS

CONTENTS

THE CD IS PLAYABLE ON ANY CD PLAYER, AND IS ALSO ENHANCED SO MAC AND PC USERS CAN ADJUST THE RECORDING TO ANY TEMPO WITHOUT CHANGING THE PITCH.

ISBN 978-1-4234-7281-0

RILTING MUSIC, INC.

EXCLUSIVELY DISTRIBUTED BY

HAL•LEONARD® CORPORATION
7777 W. BLUEMOUND RD. P.O. BOX 13819 MILWAUKEE, WI 53213

Visit Hal Leonard Online at
www.halleonard.com

ANYONE CAN WHISTLE

from ANYONE CAN WHISTLE

Words and Music by
STEPHEN SONDHEIM

HORN

BEING ALIVE
from COMPANY

3/4

HORN

Music and Lyrics by
STEPHEN SONDHEIM

Moderately

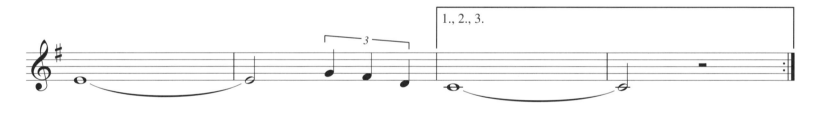

BROADWAY BABY

from FOLLIES

 5/6

HORN

Music and Lyrics by
STEPHEN SONDHEIM

5

CHILDREN WILL LISTEN

from INTO THE WOODS

7/8

HORN

Words and Music by
STEPHEN SONDHEIM

COMEDY TONIGHT

from A FUNNY THING HAPPENED ON THE WAY TO THE FORUM

Words and Music by
STEPHEN SONDHEIM

HORN

GOOD THING GOING
from MERRILY WE ROLL ALONG

Words and Music by
STEPHEN SONDHEIM

HORN

JOHANNA
from SWEENEY TODD

 13/14

HORN

Words and Music by
STEPHEN SONDHEIM

LOSING MY MIND
from FOLLIES

HORN

Music and Lyrics by
STEPHEN SONDHEIM

NOT A DAY GOES BY
from MERRILY WE ROLL ALONG

17/18

HORN

Words and Music by
STEPHEN SONDHEIM

NOT WHILE I'M AROUND

from SWEENEY TODD

Words and Music by
STEPHEN SONDHEIM

HORN

19/20

OLD FRIENDS

from MERRILY WE ROLL ALONG

HORN

Words and Music by
STEPHEN SONDHEIM

PRETTY WOMEN

from SWEENEY TODD

Words and Music by
STEPHEN SONDHEIM

HORN

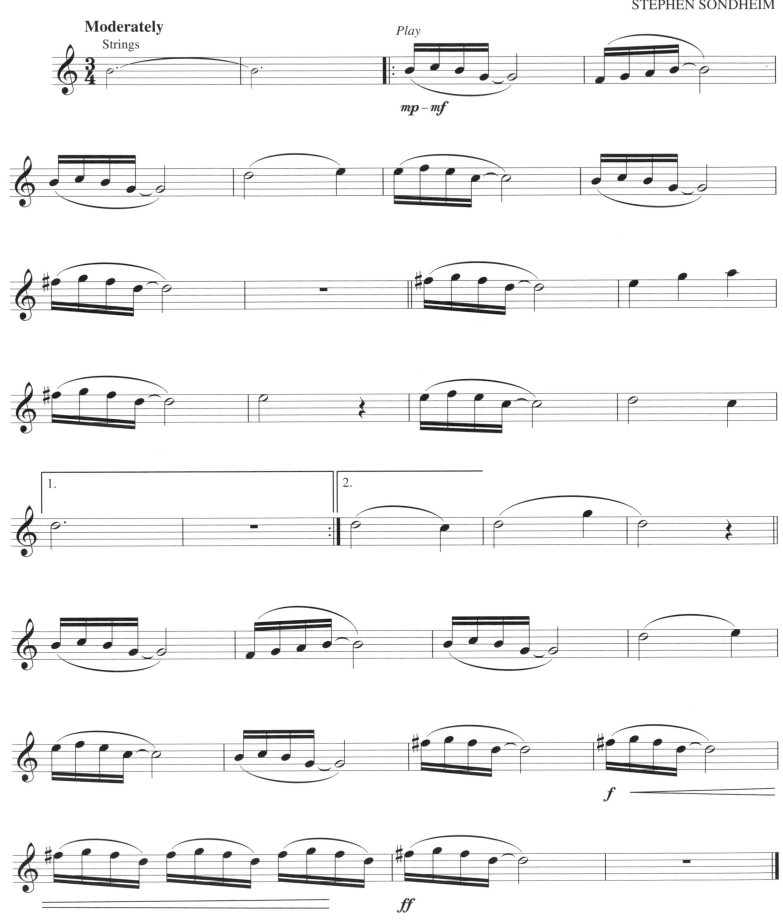

SEND IN THE CLOWNS
from the Musical A LITTLE NIGHT MUSIC

HORN

Words and Music by
STEPHEN SONDHEIM

SUNDAY

from SUNDAY IN THE PARK WITH GEORGE

Words and Music by
STEPHEN SONDHEIM

HORN